INSPIRATION

= FOR =

WRITERS

EMILY DARCY

summersdale

INSPIRATION FOR WRITERS

This revised edition copyright © Summersdale Publishers Ltd, 2017
First published in 2012

Images © Shutterstock

Summersdale Publishers Ltd
46 West Street
Chichester
West Sussex
PO19 1RP
UK

www.summersdale.com

Printed and bound in the Czech Republic

ISBN: 978-1-78685-057-7

Substantial discounts on bulk quantities of Summersdale books are available to corporations, professional associations and other organisations. For details contact general enquiries: telephone: +44 (0) 1243 771107, fax: +44 (0) 1243 786300 or email: enquiries@summersdale.com.

To....................................

From..................................

You don't write
because you want to
say something; you
write because you've
got something to say.

F. Scott Fitzgerald

WRITING IS 1 PER CENT INSPIRATION, AND 99 PER CENT ELIMINATION.

Louise Brooks

Everything in life is writable
about if you have the
outgoing guts to do it, and the
imagination to improvise.

Sylvia Plath

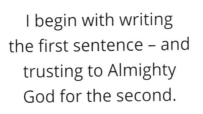

I begin with writing the first sentence – and trusting to Almighty God for the second.

Laurence Sterne

PUT IT BEFORE
THEM BRIEFLY SO
THEY WILL READ IT,
CLEARLY SO THEY
WILL APPRECIATE
IT... AND, ABOVE
ALL, ACCURATELY
SO THEY WILL
BE GUIDED BY
ITS LIGHT.

Joseph Pulitzer

One must be drenched in words, literally soaked with them, to have the right ones form themselves into the proper pattern **at the right moment.**

Hart Crane

The more important
virtue for a writer,
I believe, is self-
forgiveness.

Elizabeth Gilbert

WRITING IS THE GEOMETRY OF THE SOUL.

Plato

Writing is really
rewriting – making
the story better,
clearer, truer.

Robert Lipsyte

WHEN I WANT TO READ A BOOK, I WRITE ONE.

Benjamin Disraeli

If you want to write, you can. Fear stops most people from writing, not lack of talent, whatever that is.

Richard Rhodes

Writing is not a job description. A great deal of it is luck.

Margaret Atwood

THE LESS CONSCIOUS ONE IS OF BEING 'A WRITER', THE BETTER THE WRITING.

Pico Iyer

Write for the most intelligent, wittiest, wisest audience in the universe: write to **please yourself.**

Harlan Ellison

Writing is the
painting of
the voice.

Voltaire

LOOK IN THY HEART, AND ─ WRITE. ─

Philip Sidney

Write only if you
cannot live without
writing. Write
only what you
alone can write.

Elie Wiesel

TRY TO LEAVE OUT THE PARTS THAT READERS TEND TO SKIP.

Elmore Leonard

It is a delicious thing to write...
to be no longer yourself but
to move in an entire universe
of your own creating.

Gustave Flaubert

By writing much, one learns to write well.

Robert Southey

IF YOU CAN'T ANNOY SOMEBODY WITH WHAT YOU WRITE, I THINK THERE'S LITTLE POINT IN WRITING.

Kingsley Amis

The pen is mightier than the sword, and considerably easier to **write with.**

Marty Feldman

Every writer is a thief,
though some of us
are more clever than
others at disguising
our robberies.

Joseph Epstein

WORDS ARE A LENS TO FOCUS ONE'S MIND.

Ayn Rand

The worst thing
you write is better
than the best thing
you do not write.

Ellen Jackson

THE BEST TIME FOR PLANNING A BOOK IS WHILE YOU'RE DOING THE DISHES.

Agatha Christie

The book to read is not the one that thinks for you, but the one that makes you think.

Harper Lee

The wastebasket is a writer's best friend.

Isaac Bashevis Singer

THE EASIEST READING IS DAMNED HARD WRITING.

Thomas Hood

Yes, the story I am writing exists, written in absolutely perfect fashion, some place, in the air. All I must do is find it, **and copy it.**

Jules Renard

If my doctor told me I
had only six minutes to
live, I wouldn't brood.
I'd type a little faster.

Isaac Asimov

A WORD AFTER A WORD AFTER A WORD IS  POWER.

Margaret Atwood

All my best
thoughts were
stolen by
the ancients.

Anonymous

WRITING COMES MORE EASILY IF YOU HAVE SOMETHING TO SAY.

Sholem Asch

A man would do very well to carry a pencil in his pocket and write down the thoughts of the moment. Those that come unsought for are commonly the most valuable.

Francis Bacon

There are no laws
for the novel. There
never have been, nor
can there ever be.

Doris Lessing

THERE ARE THREE
RULES FOR WRITING
THE NOVEL.
UNFORTUNATELY,
NO ONE KNOWS
WHAT THEY ARE.

W. Somerset Maugham

I was working on
the proof of one
of my poems all
the morning, and
took out a comma.
In the afternoon
I put it back again.

Oscar Wilde

Why do
writers write?
Because
it isn't there.

Thomas Berger

THE
CHIEF GLORY
OF EVERY
PEOPLE ARISES
FROM ITS
AUTHORS.

Samuel Johnson

A writer is a person for whom writing is more difficult than it is for other people.

Thomas Mann

IMMATURE POETS IMITATE; MATURE POETS STEAL.

T. S. Eliot

I admire anybody
who has the guts to
write anything at all.

E. B. White

However great a man's natural talents may be, the art of writing cannot be learnt all at once.

Jean-Jacques Rousseau

BOOKS WANT TO BE BORN: I NEVER MAKE THEM. THEY COME TO ME AND INSIST ON BEING WRITTEN.

Samuel Butler

What no wife of a writer can ever understand is that a writer is working when he's staring out of **the window.**

Burton Rascoe

Just leave your mind alone; your intuition knows what it wants to write, so get out of the way.

Ray Bradbury

YOU CAN'T USE UP CREATIVITY. THE MORE YOU USE, THE MORE YOU HAVE.

Maya Angelou

The purpose of a writer is to keep civilisation from destroying itself.

Bernard Malamud

WRITING A BOOK IS AN ADVENTURE.

Winston Churchill

In a writer there must
always be two people – the
writer and the critic.

Leo Tolstoy

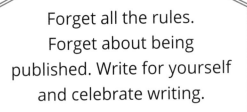

Forget all the rules.
Forget about being
published. Write for yourself
and celebrate writing.

Melinda Haynes

WRITING IS THE INCURABLE ITCH THAT POSSESSES MANY.

Juvenal

My aim is to put down on paper what I see and what I feel in the **best and simplest way.**

Ernest Hemingway

True ease in writing
comes from art,
not chance.

Alexander Pope

IF A STORY IS IN YOU, IT HAS GOT TO COME OUT.

William Faulkner

Every word born of
an inner necessity –
writing must never
be anything else.

Etty Hillesum

BECOMING THE READER IS THE ESSENCE OF BECOMING A WRITER.

John O'Hayre

As to the adjective: when
in doubt, strike it out.

Mark Twain

It is with words as with sunbeams – the more they are condensed, the deeper they burn.

Robert Southey

AN ORIGINAL
WRITER IS NOT
ONE WHO IMITATES
NOBODY, BUT ONE
WHOM NOBODY
CAN IMITATE.

François-René
de Chateaubriand

If there is a book you really want to read but it hasn't been written yet, then **you must write it.**

Toni Morrison

The faster you blurt,
the more swiftly
you write, the more
honest you are.

Ray Bradbury

TO PRODUCE A MIGHTY BOOK, YOU MUST CHOOSE A MIGHTY THEME.

Herman Melville

An author in his
book must be like
God in the universe:
present everywhere
and visible nowhere.

Gustave Flaubert

THE SECRET OF GETTING AHEAD IS GETTING STARTED.

Anonymous

Write every time you have a free minute. If you didn't behave that way you would never do anything.

John Irving

My six words of advice to writers are: 'Read, read, read, write, write, write.'

Ernest J. Gaines

**ONLY BAD WRITERS
THINK THAT
THEIR WORK IS
REALLY GOOD.**

Anne Enright

One ought only to write when one leaves a piece of one's own flesh in the inkpot, each time one **dips one's pen.**

Leo Tolstoy

Writing is the best way to talk without being interrupted.

Jules Renard

I AM ONLY REALLY ALIVE WHEN I'M WRITING.

Tennessee Williams

If you don't think there is magic in writing, you probably won't write anything magical.

Terry Brooks

WHETHER OR NOT YOU WRITE WELL, WRITE BRAVELY.

Bill Stout

Prose = words in their best
order; poetry = the best
words in their best order.

Samuel Taylor Coleridge

The role of the writer
is not to say what we
all can say, but what we
are unable to say.

Anaïs Nin

I AM NOT AT ALL IN A HUMOUR FOR WRITING; I MUST WRITE ON TILL I AM.

Jane Austen

A good style should
show no signs
of effort. What is
written should seem
a **happy accident.**

W. Somerset Maugham

We are all apprentices
in a craft where no one
ever becomes a master.

Ernest Hemingway

IF A NATION LOSES ITS STORYTELLERS, IT LOSES ITS CHILDHOOD.

Peter Handke

I'd rather be caught
holding up a bank
than stealing so much
as a two-word phrase
from another writer.

Jack Clifford Smith

YOU CAN ONLY
LEARN TO
BE A BETTER
WRITER BY
ACTUALLY
WRITING.

Doris Lessing

Better write for yourself
and have no public, than
to write for the public
and have no self.

Cyril Connolly

No author dislikes to be
edited as much as he dislikes
not to be published.

Russell Lynes

**OF ALL THOSE
ARTS IN WHICH
THE WISE EXCEL,
NATURE'S CHIEF
MASTERPIECE IS
WRITING WELL.**

John Sheffield

The greatest part of a writer's time is spent in reading in order to write: a man will turn over half a library **to make one book.**

Samuel Johnson

Writing is easy. All you do is stare at a blank sheet of paper until drops of blood form on your forehead.

Anonymous

DON'T LOAF AND INVITE INSPIRATION; LIGHT OUT AFTER IT WITH A CLUB.

Jack London

You must often make erasures if you mean to write what is worthy of being read a second time.

Horace

I'M MOST HAPPY TO BE A WRITER.

Maya Angelou

I believe one writes because
one has to create a world
in which one can live.

Anaïs Nin

Anyone can become
a writer... the trick, the
secret, is to stay a writer.

Harlan Ellison

SIT DOWN TO WRITE WHAT YOU HAVE THOUGHT, AND NOT TO THINK WHAT YOU SHALL WRITE.

William Cobbett

Of good writing
(which, essentially, is
clear thinking made
visible) precision
is **the point of
capital concern.**

Ambrose Bierce

Let who you are, what you are, what you believe, shine through every sentence you write, every piece you finish.

John Jakes

WRITE ONLY OF WHAT IS IMPORTANT AND ETERNAL.

Anton Chekhov

It is good to have
an end to journey
towards; but it is
the journey that
matters in the end.

Ursula K. Le Guin on writing

TO LIVE A CREATIVE LIFE WE MUST LOSE OUR FEAR OF BEING WRONG.

Joseph Chilton Pearce

It is an excellent discipline
for an author to feel that he
must say all he has to say in the
fewest possible words, or his
reader is sure to skip them.

John Ruskin

One resists the
invasion of armies;
one does not resist
the invasion of ideas.

Victor Hugo

NO ONE EVER, EVER GETS TO SEE DRAFT ZERO. THIS IS THE DRAFT THAT YOU WRITE TO TELL YOURSELF WHAT THE STORY IS.

Terry Pratchett
on his first drafts

No great artist ever
sees things as they
really are. If he did,
he would cease
to be **an artist.**

Oscar Wilde

The art of art, the glory of expression and the sunshine of the light of letters, is simplicity.

Walt Whitman

BOOKS
ARE THE
MIRRORS OF
THE SOUL.

Virginia Woolf

Not a wasted word.
This has been a main
point to my literary
thinking all my life.

Hunter S. Thompson

ALWAYS BE A POET, EVEN IN PROSE.

Charles Baudelaire

Not that the story need be
long, but it will take a long
while to make it short.

Henry David Thoreau

Find out what your
hero or heroine wants,
and when he or she wakes
up in the morning, just
follow him or her all day.

Ray Bradbury

POETRY CREATES THE MYTH, WHILE THE PROSE WRITER DRAWS ITS PORTRAIT.

Jean-Paul Sartre

Get it down. Take chances. It may be bad, but it's the only way you can do anything **really good.**

William Faulkner

A poet can
survive everything
but a misprint.

Oscar Wilde

WRITING IS ITS OWN REWARD.

Henry Miller

Imagination, not invention, is the supreme master of art as of life.

Joseph Conrad

GREAT IS THE ART OF BEGINNING, BUT GREATER IS THE ART OF ENDING.

Henry Wadsworth Longfellow

All the words I use in my
stories can be found in
the dictionary – it's just a
matter of arranging them.

W. Somerset Maugham

When I say I work I only mean writing. Everything else is just odd jobs.

Margaret Laurence

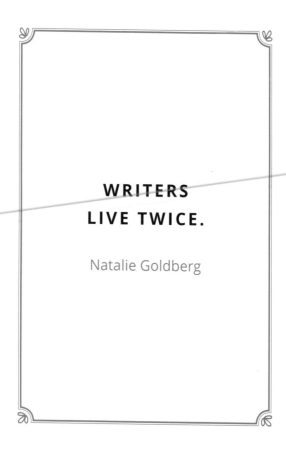

**WRITERS
LIVE TWICE.**

Natalie Goldberg

To be the kind of
writer you want to
be, you must first be
the kind of thinker
you want to be.

Ayn Rand

Don't try to figure out what other people want to hear from you; figure out what you have to say.

Barbara Kingsolver

FILL YOUR PAPER WITH THE BREATHINGS OF YOUR HEART.

William Wordsworth

To gain your own
voice you have
to forget about it
being heard.

Allen Ginsberg

STYLE IS TO FORGET ALL STYLES.

Jules Renard

The first sentence can't
be written until the final
sentence is written.

Joyce Carol Oates

The most beautiful things
are those that madness
prompts and reason writes.

André Gide

A REAL BOOK IS
NOT ONE THAT IS
READ, BUT ONE
THAT READS US.

W. H. Auden

Stories of
imagination tend
to upset those
without one.

Terry Pratchett

If I waited for perfection... I would never write a word.

Margaret Atwood ·

GOOD WRITING IS ═ REWRITING. ═

Truman Capote

A professional
writer is an amateur
who didn't quit.

Richard Bach

IN ART, ECONOMY IS ALWAYS BEAUTY.

Henry James

Every secret of a writer's soul,
every experience of his life...
every quality of his mind is
written large in his works.

Virginia Woolf

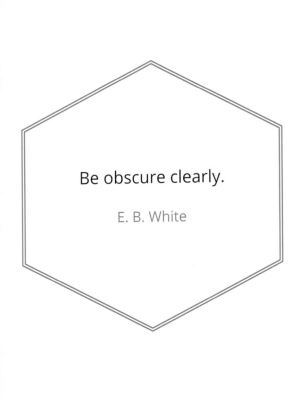

Be obscure clearly.

E. B. White

THERE IS NO GREATER AGONY THAN BEARING AN UNTOLD STORY INSIDE YOU.

Zora Neale Hurston

No tears in the writer, no tears in the reader. No surprise for the writer, no surprise **for the reader.**

Robert Frost

I can shake off
everything as I write;
my sorrows disappear,
my courage is reborn.

Anne Frank

THE
BEGINNING
IS ALWAYS
— TODAY. —

Mary Shelley

One should be
able to return to
the first sentence
of a novel and find
the resonances of
the entire work.

Gloria Naylor

CONTINUOUS IMPROVEMENT IS BETTER THAN DELAYED PERFECTION.

Anonymous

When nothing is sure,
everything is possible.

Margaret Drabble

If it sounds like writing,
I always rewrite it.

Elmore Leonard

WRITING IS EASY. ALL YOU HAVE TO DO IS CROSS OUT THE WRONG WORDS.

Mark Twain

I try to create sympathy for my characters, then turn **the monsters loose.**

Stephen King

Writing is... the place you go to inside your head. It is the imaginary friend you drink your tea with in the afternoon.

Ann Patchett

THE WORDS
OF MY BOOK
NOTHING; THE
DRIFT OF IT
EVERYTHING.

Walt Whitman

Let the world burn through you. Throw the prism light, white hot, on paper.

Ray Bradbury

DON'T QUIT – RETURN HOME TO YOUR WRITING.

Elizabeth Gilbert

Prose is architecture,
not interior decoration.

Ernest Hemingway

Don't bend; don't
water it down; don't try to
make it logical; don't edit
your own soul according
to the fashion.

Anne Rice

**ALL THAT MATTERS
IS WHAT YOU LEAVE
ON THE PAGE.**

Zadie Smith

The art of writing is
the art of discovering
what you believe.

Gustave Flaubert

If you don't have time to read, you don't have time, or the tools, to write.

Stephen King

IT AIN'T WHATCHA WRITE, IT'S THE WAY ATCHA WRITE IT.

Jack Kerouac

The more a man
writes, the more
he can write.

William Hazlitt

THERE IS CREATIVE READING AS WELL AS CREATIVE WRITING.

Ralph Waldo Emerson

Good prose is like a
window pane.

George Orwell

We write to taste
life twice: in the moment
and in retrospect.

Anaïs Nin

If you're interested in finding out more
about our books, find us on Facebook at
Summersdale Publishers and follow
us on Twitter at @Summersdale.

www.summersdale.com